Head Full of Boogeymen, Belly Full of Snakes

Poems by Jason Ryberg

Kansas City Spartan Press Missouri

Spartan Press
Kansas City, Missouri
spartanpresskc.com

Copyright © Jason Ryberg, 2020
Second Edition
ISBN: 978-1-952411-07-6
LCCN: 2020935507

Cover and interior images: Jon Lee Grafton
Back cover images: Tom Wayne
All rights reserved. No part of this publication may be
reproduced or transmitted in any form or by any means,
electronic or mechanical, including photocopying,
recording or by info retrieval system, without prior
written permission from the author.

This book was originally published as part of the Spartan Press POP Poetry Series, which ran from 2015 to 2017.

The author would like to thank the following publications in which some version of these poems originally appeared:

Rusty Truck, Kansas Time + Place, Prompts: A Spontaneous Anthology (39 West Press), *Art Uprising* (39 West Press), *Ten Foot Tall And Bullet Proof* (EMP), *The Mutiny Information Reader* (Mutiny Information Press, 2016), *U City Review, Anti Heroin Chic, The Gasconade Review, Trailer Park Quarterly, Indigent A La Carte, Rye Whiskey Review, 785 Magazine, Thimble Magazine, Ariel Charts, As It Ought To Be, The Dope Fiend Daily, Outlaw Poetry Review, Angry Old Man Magazine, Thorny Locust, Rasputin*

Special thanks to Jeanette Powers, M. Scott Douglass, Tom Wayne, Will Leathem, Jon Bidwell, Shawn Pavey, Steven H. Bridgens, The Robert J. Deuser Foundation for Libertarian Studies, The West Plaza Tomatoe Co., and the Osage Arts Community Road Team.

This book is dedicated to John Ryberg, Sr.
and Melinda Husbands Ryberg

TABLE OF CONTENTS

Ghost Out Wandering the Backroads
  (or, John Brown Returns to Kansas) / 1
The Gift of Fire (or, Kansas City
  to Raleigh in 24 Hours or Less) / 4
Sad Boy Praying for His Luck to Change (or,
  Placing a Collect Call to the Almighty Unknown) / 7
Record Skipping in a Lonely Room
  (or, My Mama Says She Loves Me
  but She Could Be Jivin', Too) / 9
They Say a Lot, Don't They? / 11
The Sudden Appearance
  of Giuseppe, the Billy Goat / 14
What Else to Do? / 16
Midnight on the Eighteenth Hole
  at the *Club Purgatorio* / 18
Drunk Man Laughing at a Silver Dollar Moon
  (or, the Night Grogger Fell off the Front Porch) / 19
Head Full of Boogeymen / Belly Full of Snakes
  (or, No Escape from the Island of Misfit Boyz) / 22

Thirteen Variations / Slight Returns
  on Dr. William's Red Wheel Barrow (or,
  How the Hell Does a Japanese Fighting Kite
  Wind up in the Middle of Missouri?) / 26

Weathervane Creaking in a Sad, Gray Wind
  (or, a Secret History of the Nighttime World) / 30

AMERICA, INC. / 33

What Is It, This Time? / 35

All of the Above / 39

Listening All Alone to Deep Purple
  in a Pittsburg Bar (Kansas, That Is) / 41

You Are Here: A Meditation on
  Phenomenology and Spiritualism
  (With a Side of Jalepenos and Mezcal) / 43

Uncle Mikey's Sunday Morning
  Gitty-up-and-Go-Go Juice / 46

Madame Leveau, Fortune Teller and Police Psychic,
  Gives One Possible Account of How It Happened / 47

The Poet's Primer for the Early 21st Century / 49

*Them that can't be killed by knives and bullets
usually break their necks fallin' off the front porch.*

-Captain Augustus McCrae, Texas Ranger

Ghost out Wandering the Backroads
(or, John Brown Returns to Kansas)

There are plenty of paintings
and a few photographs, even,
so we know someone
fitting his description
once moved amongst us
and has allegedly been witnessed,
recently, slipping in and out of
the fitful dreams of the CEOs, holy men
and politicians of Kansas (running guerilla raids
and counting coup, no doubt).

They appear to us somehow more shifty,
nervous and disingenuous than usual
and, reportedly, state-wide sales
of expensive scotches,
designer anti-depressants
and blood-pressure medications
are through the roof.

They say he observes them often from the tree-line
behind their palatial guest homes,
from bus-stop benches down on the street
across from their office parks and complexes,
from over their shoulders in the mirrors
of exclusive country club and executive washrooms:

his eyes like signal fires on distant hilltops,
like lanterns leading us through swamps and hollers
and piney backwoods on up to Freedomland *(glory be!)*,
like klieg lights calmly surveying and laying open
the meat-processing plants and voting stations
and payday loan offices and publicly subsidized
million-dollar mega-farms and mega-churches
of the over-worked, under-paid,
trans-fattened heart of The Heartland.

He has no visible means of transportation;
he is always just suddenly there and then
just as suddenly not there, and certainly doesn't possess
quite the ferocious bearing and terrifying tornadic stature
transmitted to us over the years by Curry's paintings
in the state capitol building.

Yet, there is always a quicksilver halo
of ghost fire around him,
a layer of graveyard mud on his boots
and an expertly tied noose
(with exactly thirteen knots)
hanging from his neck.

And when the time inevitably comes
to raise the question of what
it could all possibly mean,
everyone of these generous job creationists,
these steely admirals of the fleets of industry,
these selfless stewards of the souls of men,
suddenly seems to scurry away to some
dust-bowl era storm cellar
somewhere deep within themselves,

while their eyes try to focus
on some distant flittering thing
on the far, fabled horizon
of whatever's left of the 21st century
American dream.

The Gift of Fire (or, Kansas City to Raleigh in 24 Hours or Less)

for Will Leathem, Ed Tato and Mark Hennessy

The night is long and in full-effect
and there's nothing but bad radio, stale coffee
and a bright, five-battery-flashlight of a moon
that's been keeping a steady pace with us
ever since it came out from behind the clouds.

Sometime around 4am we barely miss
most of what must have been a buffalo or bear:
a meandering trail of animal and automotive viscera
visible, here and there, for nearly a mile along the road.

But we keep on keeping-on, anyway,
with a suddenly renewed and invigorated sense of purpose,
the radio low and everyone in the car suddenly
adrenalized, awake and alert for anything else
the universe might unexpectedly hurl our way
(be it deer, cop, phantom hitch-hiker
or 24-hour truck stop).

But, inevitably, we are forced to answer
nature's shrill and relentless call
and pull our (clearly ill-advised and
poorly planned) cross-country pilgrimage
over to the side of the highway
(where there surely must be
all manner of nightmarish caricatures
and creatures lurking just out of reach
of the lone, guttering torch of our dome light).

And it would appear that we have
officially arrived at that time of night
(inversely proportionate to however many miles
one is away from home and how many miles
one still has left to go)

when the far-off / way-out voices
of hell-fire preachers and UFO abductees
crackle and whisper, in and out,
of the troughs and peaks of static
foaming from the car's stereo speakers,
out and out into the great, starry firmament
surrounding us,

when the icy breath of the cosmos whispers
dirty jokes and grand unifying conspiracies
at the backs of our necks,

when unsettling thoughts and inexplicable intuitions
of eternal recurrence begin to smolder and smoke
inside our minds and we just know, somehow,
that we've all been here before, right here,
on this very spot (or one indistinguishable from it),

same time of dark, eerie, pre-dawn morning,
pissing in a ditch by the side of a highway,
and everyone of us can't help but contemplate,
however briefly, at least some of the great,
existential / metaphysical mysteries and conundrums
that have stalked our species ever since that
evolutionary leaping-off point of no return

when we discovered that for all its many gifts,
fire is still the originator of the long
snaky shadows that it casts
and causes the dark around us
to grow only
darker.

Sad Boy Praying for His Luck to Change
(or, Placing a Collect Call to the Almighty
Unknown)

We're talkin' about consulting the I-Ching.
We're talkin' about centering your chakra.
We're talkin' about the full-tilt boogie-woogie, baby.
We're talkin' about the *sho-nuff-shake-em-on-downs*.
We're talkin' about kickin' the front door in

    and takin' the back door out.

We're talkin' about knockin' the jug and ballin' the jack, Jack.
We're talkin' about burnin' with a low blue flame.
We're talkin' about gettin' every-which-way

    and lettin' the monkeys loose.

We're talkin' about gettin' ten foot tall and bullet proof.
We're talkin' about an executive session with the bottle.
We're talkin' about opening the throttle and gettin'

    real gone, gone, gone.

We're talkin' about gettin' red hot

    and ready to moan, *daddy-o.*

Yes, we're talkin' about placing a collect call
    to the almighty Unknown
which has (mostly) been known
to respond in-kind
if not always so much
with kindness.

Record Skipping in a Lonely Room
(or, My Mama Says She Loves Me
but She Could Be Jivin', Too)

9:17 in the morning,
        naked, drunk
                and bloody
like Martin Sheen in that scene
        from *Apocalypse Now*

(Saigon ... shit, still in Saigon),

one eye still pasted shut from sleep,
front and back doors wide open,
        every light in the house on,

half-eaten pizza from somewhere
I've never even heard of,

        three-quarter drained handle of
                rum,

cocaine contrails, twenty-dollar bill
and someone's Costco card

in full view on the kitchen counter
next to a Valentine's card
from my mother,

David Allen Coe's *Long Haired Red Neck*
skipping, loud, on the turn-table
for who
knows
how long...

They Say a Lot, Don't They?

They say fools look for wisdom
stamped on candy Valentine hearts
and go for long strolls
where angels bury their dead.

They say the only difference
between an angel and a demon
is the mood you catch them in.

They say rude awakenings
come to those who nod off
waiting for phones to ring.

They say women who run with wolves
often get bit on the butt.

They say men who somehow manage
to mount a tiger will only begin to fathom
the true depth of their foolishness
when they have to take a leak.

They say those who sleep under bridges
become birds in their dreams.

They say a bird in the frying pan
is worth more than big talk
from a burning bush.

They say God may not play at dice
but He? / She? / It? has been rumored
to give the old cosmic roulette wheel a spin
from time to time.

They say where God builds a megachurch
the Devil builds a fireworks / BBQ / porn emporium.

They say conspiracy is the only true religion
(in which all other religions merely play
their assigned roles).

They say he who seeks vengeance
makes two grave mistakes.

They say desires never satisfied,
ambitions thwarted, needs never met
can cause the blood to cool and the soul
to pool and blacken like grease in a trap.

They say money may be
the root of all evil
but pussy is the fruit.

    They say a lot, don't they?

They certainly do.

They certainly do.

The Sudden Appearance
of Giusseppe, the Billy Goat

And here's Giusseppe, the billy goat,
just now marauding his way onto the scene:
horn'd brow set in permanent hung-over scowl
above a fiercely territorial boogan glare,
mouth mechanically masticating on a clump of grass
like it was a big, fat wad of chaw;
a low-hanging storm cloud of pissy indignation
and simmering violence slowly cutting a broad swath
through the gossiping gaggle of chickens,
indifferent to their idiot jibber-jab
and their blustering bully-boy
alpha-rooster chaperones, as well
(shiiiiiit, those prissy, puffed-up pea brains
wouldn't even dream in their deepest,
most recessed rooster dreams
about taking a shot at him) for he is
the one, true and rightful king
of this little bump of a hill
on this little farm just outside Salina, KS.

Out of some genetic sense of reverence
and respect, no doubt,
one is automatically moved
to cover the family jewels
whenever he passes.

What Else to Do?
*with deepest apologies to the ghosts of Li Po, Tu Fu
and Su Tung Po*

Night, and the first few tentative drops
of a much-needed and long-prayed-for
summer rain going *plip, plip, plip*
down through the trees' many
cross-hatched layers of branches and leaves
to the summer-hot sidewalk below,

the trees like tattered beach umbrellas
sprouting, here and there, along the banks
of this lazy river of newly-laid tarmac,

a shy ghost in the attic window across the street,
tiny voices in the wind and grass
whispering choruses of praise (each to each)
to the Grand Schemata of Peoples / Places / Things,
the micro-cosmic minutia of it all and all other
various originators of little and large moments
of deep enlightenment, in between.

And here I am (again, it seems),
legs in *faux* lotus position, at the epicenter
of who knows how many known,
unknown and very possibly unknowable
spheres and ellipses of influence.

What else to do, then,
but raise my pint bottle up to the grinning,
blue Buddha moon to catch a view of him
through the brandy's amber luminescence
and the streaming, CinemaScopic projection
of clouds against the sky, and salute
his blissed-out, other-worldly magnificence?

My skeleton is an aching
abstract construct.

My heart is an old,
abandoned country church.

My mind is a flickering street light
at the heart of a feathery flurry
of poems that may never be finished.

Midnight on the Eighteenth Hole
at the *Club Purgatorio*

We
have finally reached
the swampy inland sea of
late June where a newly-minted
silver-dollar moon has illuminated all the
plumes and scattered wings and wind-blown
drapes of cloud that have accumulated on the ceiling of the
Royal Blue dome of heaven, drawing all their static and coin to
the surface from the deep wells of their dark and turbulent hearts.

And all the trilling, tremoloing tree frogs and basso-belching bull
frogs are out cutting heads in full force, tonight, volleying
their tribal hakas and hoodoo tunes, back and forth,
across this swollen, marshy pond, from which
the giant, cyclopean over-lord of some
alternate, inversely mirrored
underworld peers out
with a single bright
eye.

Drunk Man Laughing at a Silver Dollar Moon (or, the Night Grogger Fell off the Front Porch)

It's another sticky, windless after-hours
here in Midtown KC/MO
and the porch is all tricked-out with strings
of multi-colored lights (left up year-round
for years now, and proud of it),

and it feels as if the Great North American
Imp of the Perverse has been released
once again to practice its particular
designer / name brand of mischief here
in the dark heart of the Heartland.

And Grogger is swaying on the front porch stoop
with a beer in his hand (and an indeterminate number
in his belly), cackling Jack Nicholson / Joker style
at the face he keeps insisting he can see grinning
down at us from what we've all agreed, repeatedly,
must be the fattest, fullest, most silvery moon
any of us can ever remember seeing.

My moon! he says, *that's my moon!*

Ooooh fuck, he's all fuckered up,
we all half-amusedly / half-nervously eyeball / ESP
to each other, as he's making moves like he's actually
thinking about climbing on his bike
and pedaling his drunk ass home.

Oh, no you don't! Morales says,
but it's too little / too late as Grogger puts his foot
where there ain't no footing and *WHOOSH!, BAM!,*
he goes, ass over tea kettle, right off the ledge,
and it's a five foot drop (easy) from the porch landing,
totaling more than ten from Grogger's (unstoppable,
but thankfully helmeted) head to the (indifferent
and immovable) pavement below ...

And it's just past 2am, and the wind
is suddenly kicking-up out of nowhere,
and an ambulance is out there,
somewhere in the thick, oily hobo stew of it all,
getting closer and closer (but hey,
this is Killa City, MO, baby,
it could be heading anywhere).

And Grogger is finally coming around
as the lights and sirens are strobing and yowling
down the street (thank God they didn't bring
the ladder truck and SWAT team, this time).

But we all know he won't be *going
to no gotdamn hospital!* no matter
how much we try to reason with,
cajole or threaten him,
so we just sign the release form
and put him to bed.

And the Great North American
Imp Of The Perverse is done, here,
for the most part, and is, no doubt
needed, urgently, elsewhere.

And Grogger's moon must surely be
grinning down on us, now.

Head Full of Boogeymen / Belly Full of Snakes
(or, No Escape from the Island of Misfit Boyz)

Some nights,
the restless specter of the mind
will just not lie still,
opting instead to skulk about
the dark, gothic country-side of the psyche:
the foggy moors of the emotions,
the primeval backwoods of pre-historic memory,
the two-lane highways and old back-roads,
like stitches, criss-crossing and holding
the whole gooey, grey mass together.

On nights like these,
when the flesh (and perhaps the ego, as well)
is bruised and battered beyond recognition,
and the ancient, haunted scaffolding of the bones
is creaking and popping, like an old cedar tree in the wind,
under the compounded and constantly shifting weight
of the 60-hour work week,

when the sprawling network
of nerves and arteries and capillaries
is a NASCAR speedway (enriched by
high-octane coffee and toxic energy drinks),
the spirit searches, longingly,
for a co-sponsor, of sorts,
a technical advisor or low-grade savior, even,
to shepherd us through yet another
shadowy valley of sleepless Summer hell,

an intermediary between
the cold, indifferent cosmos
and the unreconstructed cave dweller
that still huddles, fearfully,
somewhere inside us all.

We're talking one of those nights of endless,
sexistential free-fall into the gaping, black maw
of the great Space / Time consortium,
like a city-block-sized sink-hole
just suddenly opened up beneath you,

deep and dark as the legendary
long, dark tunnel of the soul
(about which, so many poems
and stories and songs are so earnestly
purged out into the wild, blue
meme-o-sphere every year).

But here, the light at the end
is the light leaking out
from the other side of a door
left cracked open, conveniently, for you
(almost as if someone were expecting you):

a light with the weird luminescence of the light
one would dig one's own grave by, maybe,
or better yet, a prison break light
or concentration of multi-colored spot lights
shining down on you at that precise precarious moment
you've forgotten the lines to your big,
solemn, earnest speech to Life's unsmiling
and wildly indifferent grand jury.

And despite what half the ghosts in your head
and damn near every one of the snakes in your belly
are telling you, you proceed, heedlessly, anyway...

only to bolt awake, 4:37 am,
some place you don't recognize,
an old-fashioned rotary-dial telephone *ringing*
and *ringing* like a goddamn ice-pick in your ear,

a collect-call from the Island Of Misfit Boyz, it seems,

a Mr. Charley In The Box
(yeah, you remember,
you guys go *waaaay* back)

and will you accept
the charges?

Thirteen Variations / Slight Returns
on Dr. William's *Red Wheelbarrow* (or,
How the Hell Does a Japanese Fighting Kite
Wind up in the Middle of Missouri?)

apologies to W.C.W.

So much depends upon
a red tricycle left crying in the rain
beside four grinning
garden gnomes.

So much depends upon
a red Radio Flyer wagon overflowing
with tulip bulbs and garden tools,
to which a bull-mastiff pup
has been chained all day.

So much depends upon
a red windmill, doing nothing
but lazily churning
the bright blue wind.

So much depends upon
a red, rusted-out pick-up truck stuck in the weeds
(bees in its belly, mice in the muffler,
a thick forest of sunflowers in its bed).

So much depends upon
an old, red barn, barely holding up its own weight
beneath the ever-shifting weight of the seasons.

So much depends upon
a red dirt road winding its way
through the hills and valleys of Oklahoma,
beneath a storm-grey sky.

So much depends upon
a pair of faded red Chuck Taylors
hanging from a power line,
(with a bird's nest in the left).

So much depends upon
a red tail-light, barely visible on the road ahead
at five in the morning (don't ask why)
on the way to Atchison, KS.

So much depends upon
a red-gold koi, circling
the stem-like leg of a Great Blue Heron
in the middle of a stream.

So much depends upon
the foot-tall, *day-glo* red liberty spikes
on top of the tiny punk rock girl
with the baby blue Doc Martins.

So much depends upon
childhood memories
of the giant, red tomatoes
your neighbor grew every summer
in soil sown with iron filings
from his machine shop.

So much depends upon
a Red Tailed Hawk floating
on a current of wind
in a sky the color of a sky blue workshirt
that's been washed a hundred times.

So much depends upon
a red Japanese fighting kite,
wrecked and ruined in the rib-cage
of a lone Willow tree on a hill
in the middle of Missouri,

and no one, not a single soul around
to answer just one
simple fucking
question...

Weathervane Creaking in a Sad, Gray Wind
(or, a Secret History of the Nighttime World)

There's a weathervane creaking
in a sad, gray wind.

Buzzards spiraling on an invisible whirlpool
of Brownian motion, winding deeper and deeper
down to the bottom of night's mysterious inland sea.

A bed-side radio channeling old transmissions
of *The Shadow, The Lone Ranger*
and *Little Orphan Annie,*
pulling street sweepers, star quarter-backs
and bank presidents alike
back into the shallow end of sleep.

A man stepping out of the side door of his life
and into a waiting pick-up truck,
then down to the corner convenience store
for a liter of vodka and a carton of cigarettes,
(never to return).

A mysterious strain of fortune cookies
giving the fragmented (but true),
play-by-play account of what really went down
at Golgotha, Wounded Knee, Nan King,
Roanoke, Roswell, Ferguson.

A bald eagle perched on a stop light
at the corner of 39th and Bell,
KC / MO, 64111, 9:43 pm, Tuesday.

A pocket watch ticking on the end of a chain,
hanging from the rear-view mirror
of a '62 purple Impala (suicide doors,
peek-a-boo lights, Buddha on the dash-board).

A hobo sleeping in a rowboat
in a dried-up creek bed
beneath the white rose
of a cemetery moon.

A rusty railroad spike driven through
a heart-shaped box of candy, left on the front porch
of one who has not been true *(you know what you did)*.

Two freight trains passing in a foggy train yard,
like ships in a harbor, then back out
onto the high seas of the lower Midwest.

A street corner crazy
giving God and the Devil, both,
a little dose of the old *what for.*

An unknown number of
feral cats revving themselves up
to either fight or fuck.

And all the while,
a lone, melancholy moon-moth of a thought
flutters and bounces around inside
the empty Victorian opera house
of some old man's skull,
settles for a moment,
then goes back
to its manic gypsy dance
before he can catch it.

AMERICA, INC.

for Tom Wayne

Hello, you've reached the homeland offices of America, Inc.
and its various affiliated client states.

If this is an emergency, hang up and dial 9 / 11
and a response team or drone squadron will be sent
to your GPS location, immediately.

All of our operatives are currently busy assessing other
consumers, but your call is important to us and vital to our
national security, so please stay on the line.

If you think you know your political party's direct
intentions, please state them now, otherwise,
you may choose from the following menu:

for Life, Liberty and the Pursuit of Happiness, press 1,
for Truth, Justice and the American Way, press 2,
for God, Guns, Guts or Glory, press 3,
for Art vs Obscenity, press 4,

for Honor and Duty, press 5,
for Freedom and Responsibility, press 6,
for Equality Before The Law, press 7,
for Plausible Deniability, press 8,
to report suspected dissidents, drug users
or other enemies of the Homeland, press 9,
to speak to an operative, press 0, or just stay on the line.

This call is being monitored for quality assurance
as well as for your own safety and protection.

Thank you, and God bless the Homeland.

What Is It, This Time?

What is it, this time?

It's a set of elevator doors,
endlessly and randomly opening and closing
on all our various levels of perception /
conciousness / awareness / etc.

It's a slippery gateway drug
down a long helical flight
of ever-expanding co-dependencies.

It's an attic window lit with a mysterious glow
in a house where no one has lived for years
(where many a secret passageway
is rumored to silently serpentine).

What is it, this time!?

It's a hairpin turn in an already labyrinthine path
through the Garden of Earthly Delights.

It's an epic poem
folded into a leaky haiku of a boat
then set afloat on a lazy, meandering meme-stream
that runs (mostly unnoticed) through all our lives.

It's a deep, drunken mid-day nap,
ended suddenly by a dream
of wind and thunder
and a violent knocking
at the back door to which you stumble
clumsily and frantically only to find
no one there.

What is it, this time!!?

It's a midnight rendezvous
with Fate, Kharma, Kismet and Assoc's.

It's a June Bug struggling
on the floor of a bath tub
in an abandoned motel
by the side of a road you really,
really don't want to
go down.

It's a long, deep sigh let loose
like the last leaf of a dead tree
on to the frozen surface of a kiddie pool.

It's a rotting tree limb finally cracking
and falling from the accumulated weight
and misery of an ancient hangman's noose
in a forest of tall, creaking skeletons
and perpetual fog
in which too many people
have been hung.

What is it, this time!!!?

It's the lone gypsy prince of coyotes
calling up the spirits of his dead ancestors
for one last suicidal reunion tour
before the Big Bad Ragnorak*
of so many late-night campfire tales
inevitably comes rumbling, tumbling down.

It's a train broke down in a tunnel
with no light at the end.

What is it, this time!!!!?

Let me tell you what it is, *cha-cha*,
on the house and country simple,
so listen up and get it straight.

It's a priest crying with laughter
at a joke his friend the rabbi has told him
about a priest, a rabbi and a donkey
who walk into a Bar Mitzvah.

That's what it is.

Asshole.

*Ragnorak — *In Norse mythology, a series of future events, including a great battle, foretold to ultimately result in the death of a number of major figures (including the gods Odin, Thor, Týr, Freyr, Heimdallr, and Loki), the occurrence of various natural disasters, and the subsequent submersion of the world in water.*

All of the Above

A book of poems is
a family photo album
for a spectacularly disfunctional family,

a scrapbook of newspaper clippings,
wedding announcements, obituaries,
concert ticket stubs, etc, etc,

a file cabinet full of classified documents,
elaborately detailed conspiracy theories
and jealously guarded recipes.

A book of poems is
a jelly jar full of fortune cookie fortunes,

an ancient tome of forbidden knowledge,

a grimoire of (otherwise) benign
spells, hexes, hoodoos and charms.

A book of poems is (at least)
equal parts scrapyard and curio shop,
(bus station at 2am / country crossroads at midnight),

a shoebox full of old post cards
and love letters,

a rolodex of dead or merely
recommissioned phone numbers
(I'm sorry, who were you looking for?)

A book of poems is an estate sale for a wealthy,
eccentric hoarder who has been missing
and presumed dead for nearly a decade,

an operator's manual for a machine
that hasn't been invented yet,

a road atlas for a lost continent.

A book of poems is...

all of the above.

Listening All Alone to Deep Purple in a Pittsburg Bar (Kansas, That Is)

as texted to the author (more or less) by Al Ortolani

Well, there's the bartender, of course, pouring me another drink even though I've still got one in front of me (half full and un-paid for), and there's big screen tvs to the front, rear, left and right of me (no escape, apparently, so I guess I better just deal with it and have another drink) and Stevie Nicks is silently dancing in all her '80s, gypsy-black, gauzy, gossamer glory (Lord, just send me Stevie in my dreams and maybe keep all mamas and babies safe for at least one more day) and now the Red Hot Chili Peppers are really funkin' and rockin' out and the Dodgers and the Angels have hit the 7th inning (at 7 to 7, no shit, guess we'll see who gets lucky tonight) and the Goodyear blimp is in retrograde as the ghost of Kurt Cobain is coming to us live and unplugged (did he really mean to unplug and sign off for good when he arrived at his ultimate dark nadir of despair or was there something else going on there?) and I could use another drink about now and the bartender has been MIA for sometime and the conspicuous odor of pot smoke is wafting from the men's room (seriously, am I the only one noticing this!?) and there's an old gal in back who looks a lot like my mother (like unnervingly so, like one of those separated-at-birth kind of scenarios, like multiple double-checks and, seriously, what the hell would my mother be doing in a bar in Pittsburg, KS!?) saying *HELLO!? HELLO!?* into the payphone and now some old boy is moaning the Medicare blues, bent over the trashcan by the backdoor with a bloody nose, who, it turns out is an old harp player I used to know, as he sits down on the bar stool next to me *(vodka on the rocks!)* like nothing ever happened (pretty sure we chased a possum together down Broadway one night in 1995 behind the Stillwell Hotel) and I say *Hey man, you're part of my poem!* Bending his ear lower and closer to me, he says *I had a feelin'*.

You Are Here: a Meditation on Phenomenology and Spiritualism (with a Side of Jalepenos and Mezcal)
for Michael Morales

Whereas
> I'm not so much
> a full-on, absolute *denier,*
>> but really
>> more of what you might call a
>> methodological
>>> naturalist /
>
> soft-hearted atheist /
> hard-nosed agnostic (with gnostically
>> paganish proclivities
>> and a soft spot
> for the weird, fanciful and mysterious)
>> when it comes to matters concerning
> supernatural phenomena / spirit worlds /
>> higher powers / etc., etc.,
>> but if I were more
>> hard-wired that way (if not exactly
> a full-on true believer)

               and if my ratio
                       of wiring to whatever quantifiable level
      of good old fashioned
                 common credulity
           were to extend to the idea of actually
communing with and / or summoning
       said supernatural phenomena /
                           spirit worlds /
     higher powers / etc., etc., then I'd have to say
that two men of (otherwise)
                 sound mind
         sitting across a table from one another
(mano a mano, as if locked in a fierce war of wills
    on the psychic plain),
consuming raw slices
              of jalapenos and
               washing them down with shots of
     mezcal *(con gusano,* by the way,
if that makes any difference, though I don't
          know why it would) would
probably be as effective a *deus-ex-machina*
                           as any

for calling down the weird lightning

    of mystic visions

               and prophetic dreams
        and very possibly setting the cosmic
    revolving door (that is rumored to exist
        between this world and who knows
how many others),

        to spinning like

           a roulette wheel on

which

    the little black ball of the mind

                (the black pearl

        of all potential and / or accumulated

human knowledge and wisdom)

    must eventually,

        inevitably come to a rest

        (if but for

           the moment).

Uncle Mikey's Sunday Morning Gitty-up-and-Go-Go Juice

for Shawn Pavey

You will need:

a pot of coffee, black as Mississippi after midnight,
strong and dense enough to pull in the light around it,

a heaping table-spoon of Brer Rabbit Blackstrap Molasses,

a shot of I.W. Harper or Old Grandad Bonded.

Stir together and serve, scalding hot,
in a mug made from a human skull
(with a Pall Mall or Chesterfield, on the side).

Uncle Mikey says,

Remember, the coffee should be strong enough
so as the bourbon is just a little scared to climb in and
a cup or two o' this stuff make you git up and walk to town!

Madame Leveau, Fortune Teller and Police Psychic, Gives One Possible Account of How It Happened

Whereby, with much fire and lightning and thunder jumping down from great heights, Heaven did give birth to unfathomable open spaces and closed inner spaces of the dark, which, in turn, did give birth to the mountains and valleys and plains, the deep waters of the oceans with their schools of fish and sharks, its rivers running over into inland lakes, and, with many hurricanes and tornados full of rain, wind and snow did, in turn, give birth to various prototypes and earlier versions of flowers and other plants, spiders and snakes, frogs and toads, mice and rats and birds and of course their distant and lumbering cousins, the dinosaurs, which, maybe, by some combination of disease, climate change, giant rocks falling from space and the over-all inability to accommodate these things, did fade and pass away, returning to the compost heap that is (ultimately) the earth, in turn, giving birth to (or at least ushering in) the age of men and women and all their eventual (maybe even inevitable) issues, obsessions and compulsions concerning death and sex and noises in the dark, failure, success and poverty, being all alone as well as being in large crowds of other people, any number of which, at any given time, they seem to have issues with and / or are preoccupied by the constant falling in and out and in and out and in and out of love with.

The Poet's Primer for the Early 21st Century
with apologies to Harley Elliot

The Poet does his inebriated little saunter along all our
tangled barbed-wire lines of reasoning and the world's
various alphabetic avenues (drunk on wine, poetry,
virtue, what-have-you).

The Poet likes nothing better than rubbing elbows,
shoulders and frontal lobes with the hyper,
meta and sub-textual members of high, middle
and low-brow society, alike.

The Poet loves to loll about on grassy knolls,
bus stop benches and the back seats
of Cadillac convertibles, prefers not to scriven,
scrape, scurry or supplicate and can often be found
hunched and hunkered down among canebreaks
and cornrows (chowin' down on a watermelon
or stolen gooseberry pie).

The Poet carries entire constellations of on-going
conversations in the portmanteau / gutbucket of his skull,
a blowtorch song in his heart of hearts and a paperback copy
of *The Rubaiyat of Omar Khayyam* (or *Leaves of Grass*)
in his back pocket.

The Poet's pen and tongue can very often drip
with equal parts Vinegar of Snarky Irony
and Raw, Wild Honey of *Lingua Franca*.

The Poet only picks race horses with words like
mustache, hurricane, silky or *pharaoh* in their names
and delights in the lighting of candelabras
and kerosene lamps at any and all occasions.

The Poet chops and chops at the uncarved block
at the dark heart of the forest primeval of the world
only to come upon it, incredulously, again and again,
each morning, completely reformed.

The Poet voluntarily faces the wildly indifferent
firing squads of a post-post-literate society with eyes
wide open and a cigar in her mouth, finds the Good,

Just and Beautiful in the most unlikely places,
stops traffic to rescue turtles and shatters all previous
world records for juggling chainsaws and *number of
metal spoons magnetized to the body.*

The Poet discovers, routinely, that it's all been discovered
before / heard before / said before yet still needs to be
re-examined, re-interpreted and re-packaged every time.

The Poet sits, covered in the early morning dew of 4am,
listening to the glistening blades of Blue Stem,
Purple Top and Goat Grass, insisting to the rest
of the tribe that she can hear it growing all around us.

The Poet stinks just a little too much, sometimes,
of the smoky, smouldering compost heap
of his own compounded yearning.

The Poet often soars too close to the sun (much
in the same way as the moth to the bug zapper)
on wings made of duct-tape, cardboard and coathangers,
only to be reborn every morning at the bottom of the sea
and wash ashore to do it all again and again and again...

The Poet refuses to cooperate or incriminate,
can neither confirm nor deny, is *currently unaware
of any such activity or operation, nor would they be
disposed to discuss such an operation
if it did in fact exist (sir).*

And always, always
The Poet swears that they'll never fall
for the same old, tired, bullshit routines and yet,

here we are again…

www.ingramcontent.com/pod-product-compliance
Lightning Source LLC
Chambersburg PA
CBHW030138100526
44592CB00011B/939